The Isles of Scilly:

Britain's Most Amazing Islands

A Personal View From A Fourth Division Tourist

Alan Peters

Contents

Contents 2

Introduction 4

Chapter One: The First Time 7

Chapter Two: St Mary's 12

Chapter Three: The Twelve Best Places To Eat On Scilly 23

Chapter Four: The Off Islands 37

Chapter Five: Our Own Odyssey 50

Chapter Six: Twelve Things You Have to Do on Scilly 69

Chapter Seven: Everything Else 97

Chapter Eight – Some Final Words 106

© Copyright 2017 by …… - All rights reserved.

It is not legal to reproduce, duplicate, or transmit any part of this document in either electronic means or in printed format. Recording of this publication is strictly prohibited.

Other books by Alan Peters

AJ Rutherford's Russian World Cup in Russia – a comic look at the 2018 World Cup through the eyes of that well known (in his eyes) pundit, AJ Rutherford. 'Funny and Moving'

Dib Dabs, Allegros and Loving They Neighbour. Memoirs of a 70s boy. Nostalgic and evocative recollections of growing up in the 1970s, perfect for any 50 or 60 something.

Blaize – Exciting children's and teens' fiction recounting the time travels of a reluctant Blaize Jackson. Perfect for any kid (or adult) that loves time travel drama.

These are all available via Amazon, or visit www.abpetersfreelancer.co.uk for more information.

Introduction

Thanks for buying this book. For those who have never visited the islands, or whose only experience was a nausea inducing day trip on the Scillonian, I hope that you will be encouraged to take a proper holiday there. There is so much more to the islands than a brief sit on Town beach, dreading the time when you need to re-board the boat, might lead you to believe.

Name the view

For more experienced holiday makers, I hope that you learn something new, get a number of ideas for something different to do on your next visit and appreciate some of the opinions offered.

That leads me to the point that this is a very personal book. By Scilly tourist standards, I am something of a newbie. Last summer represented the tenth consecutive year for our family. By Scilly standards, that is nothing.

Stuck at Newquay airport (more on that later) I thought I'd impress a couple of teenagers who were, like us, facing the consequences of a cancelled flight.

'It's our tenth year.' I told them proudly. They didn't seem impressed.

'Yes, we come every summer,' replied the girl, who was in charge of her younger brother. 'It's my thirteenth. Unlucky I guess.' She nodded towards the driving rain fogging the picture windows. 'Well, thirteen I can remember. The first four, I was too young for them to make much of an impression.'

This is a girl who has probably never voted in an election, and can't drink in a pub. But she was on her seventeenth visit.

So, please read on. You'll see some personal takes on the inhabited islands, and a little bit about some of the unpopulated ones as well.

You'll learn about aspects of the history – ancient and more recent – of this amazing place, and some views on places to eat, sites to visit, things to do. There will be some stories, a little bit from the wife (a proper holiday maker, she's been coming, on and off, for thirty years. Not top division, of course, but definitely better than my own mere ten summers.)

And, also, some thoughts from the younger members of the family.

It's a gentle book, and should hopefully make you smile and get the time to pass a little more quickly than might be the norm.

A bit like the Isles of Scilly, in fact.

Relaxing on Tresco. Personally, I think the idea of getting both feet up is too much hassle

Chapter One: The First Time

When she was a baby, our eldest had a bit of an issue about sand. Number Two had no such problem, and consumed it with a relish that we did not feel when, a couple of hours later, it appeared in her nappy.

But Number One didn't like it. We discovered this on Shanklin beach, on the Isle of Wight.

Nine months old, encased in whole body sun protection suit – we used it to help keep out the cold more than the sun, we are talking about Shanklin, after all – she was sat on a beach mat, happy enough to suck on a teething ring.

Then her foot moved, just enough for the only uncovered part other than her head, that is her toes, to encounter the grainy substance.

'Noooooo' the cry was heart breaking, and her foot retreated from the sand like a periwinkle shrivelling away from a toddler's hand. She gave a look that would not be repeated until her MMR months later – a look that said: 'You are my parents and you have betrayed me.'

It was heart-breaking. People looked up from their flasks of tea and teenagers' heads poked out of hoodies.

So, when our second popped out a couple of summers later, we thought that holidays would consist of city tours and pebble beaches. Days of sun and sand were, at least for the next few summers, out of question.

But Birmingham and Bognor can provide only temporary relief from the drudge of daily existence, and so, when Number Two was two, we bit the bullet, booked a flight and headed off for the islands.

That was the first challenge, we soon discovered. Our last hotel holiday had been pre-children, Wifey and I felt that we all needed the flexibility of self-catering. The chance to return home when the girls were tired, or we were, and having everything on hand to mash bananas and cook pasta was far more attractive than a hotel room. Plus, two weeks without a washing machine was a complete non-starter.

And, we couldn't afford a hotel, not that this influenced our decision. After all, who would take up the option of meals provided and washing up done when we could do it ourselves?

But finding a place for the first time was tricky. Everywhere was booked up, and the odd place that wasn't was one of:

- miles from the town (anybody who has ever been to the islands will know that to be an over-exaggeration, but don't forget, we had a toddler) or

- horrifically expensive (anybody who has ever stayed in one of the Garrison houses will know that to be an under-exaggeration) or
- on hold for the guests who came every year so didn't bother to book until the last minute.

In the end, we found a house, somewhere a little larger than we needed, by the Chapel on the way out of town. Well Cross was a three-bedroomed house and actually in budget. It seemed wonderful. And was.

OK, we were Well Cross when the owner rang to say that there had been a double booking, but he soon sorted that. We would soon learn that little flustered a Scillonian.

The next challenge was how to get there. As I said earlier, Wifey was a regular traveller to the islands, and so had endured the Scillonian (a boat whose bark is, I think, actually much worse than its bite) and absolutely swore she would never vomit on it again. Since she knew that throwing up was compulsory, at least for her, she swore the Scillonian was out of the question.

But trust me, it really isn't that bad. Honestly. Truly… and I say this not just because we are dependent on The Isles of Scilly Steamship Group to get us to the islands, which they have done, successfully and politely every year (mostly).

Getting on a helicopter (they flew in those days) would mean a six or seven-hour drive – that was beyond us all, with a toddler and a five-year-old.

We were well happy with Well Cross

Or, a flight from Southampton airport – I am getting nostalgic just writing about that – a mere 90 minutes from home.

Perfect. It meant, admittedly, that said two-year-old would not have her push chair, or high chair or most of the other essentials that a family loads whenever taking a little one on a journey further than the local supermarket.

But she'd cope. They both would.

And so, our family adventures began. I can't remember much of that first year. There was a lot of carrying of children down to the harbour, and we couldn't have managed without the assistant boat men who passed Number Two across from one parent to another.

Number One discovered that the Scilly sand was more agreeable than that of Shanklin, and was happy to run over the white fragments with the best of them. Number Two had, by now, outgrown the nutritional value of sand, although was still partial to the odd mouthful when she thought that nobody was looking.

She can't remember anything of that first trip, but our teenager has some vivid recollections. She remembers far more than I (but then, we have a history of memory problems down my family line) and my wife. She remembers an under stairs toy store, and buckets and spades left outside.

She remembers the Bishop and Wolf (for newcomers, one of the islands' pubs) and its barman who would entertain her and her sister by calling them Trouble and Pickle. Names he would recall for years to come, much to their delight. She remembers stepping on St Agnes for the first time.

But what we all recall was a great holiday, and our destination for the future was decided.

Chapter Two: St Mary's

We have always stayed on St Mary's. It is a metropolis – airport, quay, supermarket, Oxford Street of shops, bus service, hospital…ummm, secondary school. And, have I mentioned the airport and bus service?

In eight of our ten visits as a family, we have stayed in the Old Customs House. Smuggling must have been a bit of a problem on Scilly in the past, because in fact there are two Old Customs Houses. One is grandish affair close to the Holman's Green where you can overlook the beach and harbour, while eating an ice cream, or watching children engage in mixed martial arts with the herring gull population.

Post Office Arch – Our Old Customs House is tucked away just through here

But we go for the more central of the two. Both are in the island's main conurbation, Hugh Town, the centre of which is, to us tourists at least, the Co-op. The more visible of the two Old Customs Houses, the one near the green, is a good 100 yards from the co-op, which means it is distinctly suburban when it comes to Hugh Town, but our former coastal watchtower is right in the heart of the city.

Our morning journey for croissant involves a staircase, a dash under the famous post office arch (see left) and eight steps to cross the road. Then we are there. It means we can get a proper choice of pastries before they are gobbled up by the adventurous sorts who spend the night docked in the harbour.

Lynne Thomas is our landlady, a lovely Scillonian who is a wealth of knowledge about the islands, and particularly its comings and goings. She lives in a downstairs apartment while we take two weeks over two floors in the upstairs duplex.

It was there, in fact, where we discovered the most astonishingly boring board game ever invented. It is called Exploration, and is amazingly complex. Players collect equipment and manpower before setting off to explore mountains, ancient lands and seas, collecting goodies on their way. Now, as you will imagine, preparing for such a real adventure would take months, even years, of preparation, plus weeks of travel, search and return. Trust me, this game seems as though it is played in real time.

What makes the game so extraordinary is the dice. Rather than a normal 1-6 on each face, this particular cube features mysterious signs. Even after eight years of play, the instructions each face represents are so complex we still have to sit with rule book by our side to interpret at least one in six throws.

And after you have worked out what you do, you move your piece. The board is enormous, and divided into tiny squares. Each explorer needs to get to a far corner and back to the base in order to complete their game, but the dice allows a maximum of two squares to be navigated, and frequently the complex instructions mean that you can't actually move at all.

But there is something about the game. It is like watching a five-day test match, or the best of 37 final of world snooker, or even an election night broadcast.

After your initial boredom, the game kind of opens up, and a fascination develops which makes Exploration addictive. Like heroine, or gambling. Wifey doesn't agree, but the rest of us look forward to the rainy afternoon when Exploration will appear from under Lynne's upstairs TV to be played.

Some years, we have even pretended to see rain, just to have an excuse to play.

Daughter number one is the main fan, and even purchased a box from eBay. For extremely unsurprising reasons, the game is no longer available new today. But, for around £20, you can get your own version. You could even buy ours, because, like cheap

French wine, it is a joy best experienced in its home location. In our case, that is on Scilly. We have never opened our own family box.

But this chapter is supposed to be about St Mary's, so let's get back to there.

St Mary's grows and shrinks with the tide. Four small off islands connect and move away as the sea comes in and out.

The best of these, we think, is Toll's Island. This small piece of land is big enough to sustain plenty of vegetation, and is accessed via the astonishingly beautiful Pelistry Bay beach. From here, you can see the mainland on a clear day, watch the Scillonian sway its way in and see the Jumbos come in to land at the airport.

A little note about the planes on Scilly. There are three varieties, two of which are run by Skybus, a kind of small scale British Airways. Skybus is also the Isles of Scilly Transport Company, as far as we can make out. It runs not only the planes, but the Scillonian and the cargo ship that supports the islands.

The other variety of plane are the tiny propeller driven private aircraft owned by the rich who love the islands. If enough of you buy this book, that might include me. I promise, absolutely, to give you free flights if I ever achieve that status, and my fingers are only slightly crossed behind my back. So, recommend what you are reading to your friends, family, neighbours, work colleagues, strangers – in fact, sing it from your window. But, just for once, I digress.

Skybus operate two types of aircraft – the mid-sized, BN2 Islander, which carries eight passengers. And the jumbo. It is widely believed that the makers of the Boeing 747 stole the nickname of their aircraft from Skybus' major transport vehicle, the DHC-Twin Otter, or jumbo as we call it, which, when full, carries two pilots and seventeen passengers plus, as long as it isn't too big, a dog.

You might expect such a small plane to offer little in the way of on board entertainment, but get an aisle seat and you can look over the pilots' shoulder, see them twiddle alarmingly with switches and a large overhead lever (I'm not sure what it does, but they play with it constantly) and even watch planes cross your flight path on the on board radar.

Sometimes, when the little aircraft shape becomes a little too close, the pilots will lean forward, and scan the sky urgently. They might only be looking for rare migrating birds, but whatever, it adds a frisson of excitement.

The operator used to fly from Bristol, Southampton, Exeter, Newquay and Land's End, but since the ending of the helicopters the first two are off the agenda, which is a nuisance for us.

Inside a Jumbo, not many planes where you can look out the cockpit

They should have thought of that when changing their schedules.

We fly now from Exeter, which can be an experience, much in the same way as being trapped on Everest might be described as an experience (I hasten to add, any criticism here, or later in this book, is resolved solely for Exeter Airport, not Skybus. And I say this BEFORE I get the free flights). But, for all the potential negatives, seeing the islands for the first time from 5000 feet is a sight to behold.

There are no better views in Britain, and in their way, the world.

The sight might not be as dramatic as seeing the Victoria Falls, or flying over the Grand Canyon, but that is the point.

Scilly is about moderation. In all things. And within that sphere, it is without challenge as the most wonderful place possible to imagine.

But back to Pelistry and Toll's Island.

The land bridge connecting the two takes some navigating, and is dangerous when covered by the sea as the tides rip violently and are capable of dragging the unwary inches off course (no, seriously, swimming to Toll's Island is not recommended, unless you are one of the numerous seals that come to watch the human zoo on the beach).

But when the tide is out, and plenty of preparations have been undertaken – survival bag, letting at least four people know your plans, emergency flares and a couple of days rations just in case, the crossing can be completed, by the fit, in less than an hour. About fifty-nine and a half minutes less than an hour.

The view from Pelistry, and Toll's island is, as I have said, stunning. The Eastern Isles (not the most dramatic, but definitely the prettiest) are close by and the expanse of sea beyond is breathtaking.

It is no surprise that the frequent cruise ships that disgorge their cargo for stop overs frequently come to rest off Pelistry. Although, the shallowness of the sea closer to the harbour might also play its part.

But what else on the island? Well, it has cars and once, for a short period, a set of traffic lights were installed.

They were only temporary, although I seem to recall their arrival made the national press, and were there while the airport was being updated – I think they put a runway and security in. Whatever, the friendly staff, excellent café and views make St Mary's airport the world's finest.

The island has three A roads, although I can't recall any white lines marking the centre points. The total length of the roads combined almost reaches double figures, and the main ones can be explored on a tour bus or by vintage car.

You could even walk, although if doing so it's probably more fun to stick to the coastal paths. Something of the naughty schoolchild is evoked when you walk round the southern extremities to suddenly find yourself on the airport runway as the 10.55 from Exeter drops to land in over the cliff.

I did read somewhere that Heathrow were thinking of opening up their runways in a similar way.

Back to the roads, another way for tourists to explore is by hiring a golf cart, but more of this later. Alternatively, you can catch the island's bus.

This is brilliant if you want to get back from, say, Pelistry to Hugh Town after a hearty lunch at the Carn Vean and don't fancy the up and down trek walking would involve.

The bus used to advertise a Burnley solicitor in its window, and the doors would open by driver Steve Sims tugging on a piece of string. But in 2013, things changed when the old bus retired and a new (ish) Mercedes took its place.

It will take you through the major communities of the St Mary's land mass. From Hugh town, out towards the golf club and up to Telegraph. On to Maypole, along to Pelistry and Normandy before dropping down into Old Town and through the suburbs back to the Metropolis.

Telegraph features my dream house, a round tower with 360 degree views from the top. We look every year in the hope that it has gone on the vibrant housing market, where houses sometimes sell.

Steve used to have a second job – he may still do, but if so, we haven't heard him advertise for a while.

Scilly has its own radio station, and Steve would present a music show interspersed with chat he recorded with users of his bus. We took part one year, following a request for material for his programme, and were subjected to an in-depth interview about our views on the islands. The reward was to choose a record Steve would play in his show. We had just been, as a family, to see a production of the Andrew Lloyd Webber and Tim Rice classic, Jesus Christ Superstar, and so, after much debate (which, fortunately, wasn't aired) chose Hosanna from the show.

Steve possesses the dry wit of the Scillonian, and we were subjected to much humorous mickey taking on the radio, before he managed to play the most awful version of this uplifting and meaningful piece. We could only presume it was from an amateur production he had discovered on YouTube.

What else on St Mary's? Some of the attractions will feature in another chapter, but walking, enjoying the many beaches and visiting galleries must rate highly.

The best beaches are, in our opinions, Pelistry, as explained above. Porthcressa, which looks south from Hugh Town, and has a small but perfectly formed playground at one end, and brilliant rocks to climb at the other. We also like to eat ice creams sitting on a bench overlooking Town Beach, which is the other side of Hugh Town overlooking the quay and harbour.

Old Town Beach is our other regular haunt, laying back against the sea wall, with rocky views and the medieval, but no longer used, quay crumbling slowly to oblivion.

There are many others, and were we to visit them all, possibly our list might change. There are some superb white sandy places to the north, and others, such as Porth Hellick with its resident camel and plaque to a famous Naval chief. Some of you might think you prefer these to our choices. But we know best, so follow our advice.

Some online commentary suggests that a flaw of Scilly is its choice of eating places. We strongly disagree – indeed Number

One anticipates return to the islands for a whole year, looking forward to one particular dish. In the next chapter, my family and I will feature the ten best places to eat on the islands. I am not sure how many Michelin Stars are shared amongst the eateries listed, but if quality was measured in Peters' Planets, then a whole solar system would feature in the next chapter.

The main island of Scilly

Chapter Three: The Twelve Best Places To Eat On Scilly

I shall start with an apology. We haven't visited all of the places to eat on Scilly – the children tend to like what they like and we stick to those options. So, we have never purchased a meal to reheat from the Tanglewood Kitchen Company; only once have we found the pancake kiosk open at a time we were on Porthcressa Beach. We haven't visited Tolman's Café for a while, since discovering that their array of amazing cakes was gone, incurring a family boycott. (Hint here to the owners, in case they are reading this book).

And we have only once been to an off island (the name for the smaller inhabited islands) in the evening, so it is mostly just lunches we can judge from those. Apologies to the landladies, landlords and maître ds of St Agnes, Bryher, St Martin's and Tresco.

Juliet's Restaurant, out towards the golf club on the main island, we see as just too far to walk, especially with the hill at the end, and we are too tight to pay for a taxi.

Other places, such as the Old Town Pub, Spiros and such like we have never visited for no particular reason. They are, I am sure, as superb as the remainder of the island's take aways and eateries, but, I'm sorry, they don't feature here.

We also had two absolutely stunning meals at the St Mary's Hall hotel, but one that was very disappointing, when we were dumped in the bar having booked the restaurant. We are an unforgiving family. Sorry.

Twelve - The Farm Deli, Hugh Town, St Mary's

A wide selection of local produce and some fancy foods can be purchased from here. However, it makes our top twelve on the back of its coffee (me) and hot chocolate (everybody else).

Sumptuous Americanos offer an occasionally needed reminder of mainland civilisation (don't worry, any nostalgia is fleeting), and creamy cappuccinos are great for the afternoon, when an ice cream doesn't appeal.

The hot chocolates are worthy of an architectural award. In fact, when all the members of the family wanted one, I had to make two journeys (fortunately, as I said earlier, The Old Custom's House is very central, and so is the Farm Deli.) Lovely hot chocolate, lashings of cream and marshmallow are just what the captain ordered when the Atlantic fronts are rolling in.

The Deli also sells a good array of freshly made cakes, and some of the best quiche I have eaten. It makes a perfect picnic lunch if the plan is to spend the day on one of the uninhabited islands. I don't want to take business away from the co-op – it's the only place to get good pain au chocolat first thing in the morning – but when it comes to a takeaway lunch, there is only one contender.

Eleven – The Chip Van, Town Beach, Hugh Town

As you would imagine, fish and chips feature highly on the menus of many of the islands' eateries. The chip van, which is open early evening, is a treat. A big part of the pleasure is judging the time to go. The crowds begin to gather, a bit like they might in an Italian Square, and waiting time can be up to 45 minutes – even longer if you judge it badly.

But that is a part of the pleasure. Porthcressa beach is just behind you, and you can spend the time chatting with locals or other holiday makers, or simply enjoying the view and breeze. There is a pleasure in hearing names called out, and seeing the queuing throngs in front of you diminish, while you look with sympathy on newcomers.

And you know that your food is really fresh. Number One eats a lot of fish and chips on the island, and rates the van in her top three providers. Praise indeed.

Looking out from Little Arthur's Café

Ten – Fraggle Rock, Bryher

This is Bryher's only pub, although there are alternatives for those seeking a non-alcoholic setting.

Fraggle Rock is a three in one pub. Outside, elegant seats and tables rest beneath giant umbrellas, and when the sun shines, it really gets trapped there. One could almost be in the Caribbean. We tend to lunch early on the off islands, and that means we can usually get a table, although they fill up quickly.

Inside downstairs is a traditional pub, with pool table, small bar and toilets which, in the men's at least, feature a signed picture from Birds of a Feather stars Linda Robson and Pauline Quirk.

Then upstairs, it is as though Notting Hill has transferred to a little island off the coast of Cornwall.

Here, gastro pub reigns, with shiny surfaces, designer crisps and flashy pumps.

The food is good, I tend to go for a cheese sandwich which often comes with a nice chutney. Wife and daughter number two will go for a tuna sandwich, and Number One a bowl of chips.

We live it up on Scilly, as you can see.

Nine – Bishop and Wolf, Hugh Town, St Marys

The Bishop and Wolf provides a hint of the unknown, one year it will blow the mind with brilliant batter on the fish and chips, some good plainish pasta dishes which Number Two favours, and a good array of burgers, chilli and the like.

At other times, it is less good. Go upstairs if you haven't been there yet. You can spend your leisurely wait for food debating the colour of the walls. Light yellow, I think, whilst the others go for pale lime green. It probably depends on where the light comes from. But it is an important debate, and one I do feel sometimes does not get the attention it deserves. Not even on Scilly.

That's another thing about Scilly. Matters such as whether President Trump is going to blow up the world, or what the daily lies around Brexit might be are important (perhaps more so the first). But they tend to get lost. Maybe not for the locals, but certainly for us tourists. The colour of the Bishop and Wolf walls becomes much more important than even the latest football transfer news.

One thing about the Bishop (as we almost locals like to call it) is that there will usually be a surprise or two. Last time we went they had installed a kind of beeper, rather like a hospital pager, which went off every time a meal was ready. Since this was, in a busy place, about every 90 seconds, it did become somewhat intrusive. Sometimes, the restaurant part, upstairs, is open, sometimes not; occasionally a little side room off the main bar will host diners, other times it is closed.

There's always, you see, a touch of wonder when eating here.

Most astonishing the last time we went were the minted peas. Maybe I am gastronomically ignorant, but never before had I come across minted peas that seemed to be no more than peas covered with mint sauce, the type normally reserved for lamb.

The thing is, though, they were the best minted peas I had ever eaten.

Eight – Little Arthur's Café, Higher Town, St Martins

This is the eco café of the islands. Vines grow inside the dining hall, and you can book your own eco cottage in which to stay.

There is a tremendously rustic feel to the food. Massive but exquisite home-made rolls, and the best cheese and chutney filling; brilliant hot chocolate (daughters sometimes have one instead of food, such is their size) and the best cola in the world.

I don't think that they make this themselves, and I am not sure of the brand – certainly, I have never seen it in home supermarkets. They also offer drinks like rose lemonade and a rather fine elderberry presse.

Maybe it is the time we go, which is early for lunch, but it seems one of the islands' best kept secrets, does this, as it sits halfway up the hill to Higher Town, overlooking the beautiful Little Arthur Island (one of the Eastern Isles which can be viewed from a different perspective on Pelistry Beach). I cannot recall ever struggling for a table, and usually there are only one or two others there when we are.

Tourists don't know what they are missing.

Seven – Pom's Thai Takeaway, Town Beach, St Mary's

One of the reasons that the Fish and Chip van didn't come higher up this personal family list is that, while Wifey and Number One have their fish and chips, Number Two and I await our Pom's Thai takeaway. The other two don't really like Thai food, but I can tell you (and I carry more weight than the others) that this is possibly the best Thai food you will ever consume.

It comes with a freshness that almost hurts. The food is prepared as ordered by Mrs, presumably, Pom while her assistant (he also made our amazing Deli hot chocolates) takes orders. That she can produce such scintillating spicy tastes from a small van is quite incredible.

The Turk's Head, St Agnes – Britain's most south westerly pub

Six – Turk's Head, St Agnes

The Turk's Head is Britain's most South Westerly pub. It is extremely popular, and during the tourist season boats run so that St Mary's citizens of the permanent and temporary kind can experience its evening meals.

It changed hands recently, and became a touch too gastro for our tastes, but hopefully that will change. To us, it was renowned for fresh and tasty ploughman's, simple pasta and brilliant bread. Last time, the bread was bit too, how to put it politely, home-made and the pasta didn't always feature with its simple tomato sauce.

But despite this, the joy of sitting at a simple bench, overlooking the bay and feeding the endless sparrows takes some beating. The sun always shines on St Agnes; it appears as the most tropical of the islands, and with the islands' only deep-water channel separating it from most of the others, it is a bit different.

The Turk's Head rightly cashes in on that, and remains one of our favourite places. Just, please, simplify the bread.

Five – Anywhere That Sells Troy Town Ice Cream

It is, simply, the best. This might be unfair to other small gelato makers around the country, but we are biased. Most days will feature, at some point, a cone or tub of one of the many flavours. Apparently, there are thirty to choose from.

And a little like playing Exploration, the environment adds to the flavour.

(Actually, there is a little place near Milton Keynes, an artisan ice cream maker called Marriott's whose lime and coconut flavour comes, like Leicester City FC, from nowhere to steal the title. If you are dining in North Bucks, find out if it is for sale – it is quite amazing.)

Four – The Mermaid, Hugh Town

Sit in its dining room and the doors open directly onto the sea – the unlikely event of a sudden wave in the harbour would soak you from top to toe. That would be less comforting than the head to foot glow a pint of Tribute Ale and a meal at the Mermaid offers.

If the children's votes were permitted to count for more, then the Mermaid would be a position higher, because its fish and chips are almost without parallel (sadly for them, they have to compete with the premier provider of the nation's most traditional favourite dish).

But the Mermaid is a pub that also offers a great array of other dishes, with extremely reliable quality. Booking is recommended, we have sometimes squeezed in on the day, but more often have been turned away.

To get to the fresh and open dining room, eaters pass through a very traditional pub, which always seem to be packed with pool players and locals.

Three – The Ruined Beach Café, Raven Porth, Old Grimsby, Tresco

Book or get there early. Judging by the number of daily boats to Tresco, it is the most popular of the off islands and most seem to make their way to this fabulous, beach side restaurant,

If you can, sit in one of the sun catching outside booths, created by natural foliage.

Should those paragraphs sound a bit like they should live in a holiday brochure, then apologies, but The Ruined Beach Café's food is marvellous, especially the wood fired pizzas.

I have to be honest, it is more popular with Wife and I than the children, although they still like it, and perhaps that is partly because we love looking out onto a splendid beach below, with castle ruins on the nearby hills

Tresco exudes wealth, it is alone among the islands for that. Sometimes it seems just a little too classy, a little too manufactured, like a minimalist sitting room in white where style supersedes comfort.

That very much does not apply to this foodie heaven.

Two – The Galley, Hugh Town

Number one for restaurants, you will definitely need to book to get a meal at The Galley. We signed in as soon as we arrived, and still had to wait a week for the first vacant space. We booked our second meal straight away.

The Galley is small, maybe eight or nine tables, each full of eagerly awaiting customers. It is a fish restaurant, and offers the most delicate fish and chips. If you can, go twice, have this dish the first time, and on the second, try something different. But make sure it involves fish.

I had, on my second visit, the most exquisite curry, the creamy sauce enhancing, not swallowing, the delicate flavours. Service is good, and there is plenty of wine to choose from, by the glass as well as bottle, which always helps.

Desserts are also delicious, which is not always something true on the islands – perhaps a difficulty in getting fresh ingredients limits choice. Book and enjoy. An absolute must.

One – The Carn Vean

Lunches only here, but there are four special reasons for these outstanding tea rooms coming in at number one.

Firstly, it does the finest tuna sandwiches money can buy. I know, because this is Number One's (daughter, not restaurant) food speciality. Indeed, the year in our house is measured not in weeks or months but in PCV and ACV (days past and approaching Carn Vean).

About mid-January the P turns to the A, as we start the count down to the next visit.

Secondly, The Carn Vean does the best cakes. The very best. Anywhere. In the world. Misunderstand my point here at your peril. The most excellent, ever. If the cook ever appears on Bake Off, they can just forget the programme. The competition is over.

I trust I am clear on this.

The Gluten Free Chocolate Cake (capitals absolutely necessary) is Number Two's absolute favourite, and she is an expert when it comes to chocolate cake. Personally, I alternate between the Chocolate Orange Sponge and Bakewell Tart. Wifey tends to go for something chocolatey and crispy while Number One is normally too full from the tuna sandwiches to eat more, but will sometimes share something with her mum.

Thirdly, the lady behind the desk is the kindest, nicest, person you will ever meet. Number two still talks about the sweets that were bought to her when, on the last day of our holiday, they ran out of chocolate cake.

And finally, the Carn Vean forms a part of the perfect day. A gentle stroll to Pelistry, a five-minute walk to the café then an exciting bus ride back or, sometimes, a stroll home via Old Town and an ice cream.

You see, I hope, that this is the thing about Scilly. Read the restaurant reviews and, when the writers occasionally put on the Kevlar and venture out of London, they still head for some centre of population.

Then they rave about the pig's trotters soaked in Earl Grey tea and soapsuds, or the saffron infused calves brain flavoured ice-cream when the perfect day's meals are a stunning sandwich and piece of cake for lunch, and fish and chips for dinner.

At least, they are to us. And that's what counts.

The World's best tuna sandwiches and chocolate cake are available here

Chapter Four: The Off Islands

Tresco – the Glamorous Island

Tresco is, of course, famous for its Abbey Gardens, but the only time we went was on our very first, pre-marriage, trip to the Islands. I can't remember much about them, although I am sure that they are wonderful.

No, to us, Tresco is about other things. Hiring a bike, falling off it, lunch at the Ruin Beach Café, walking across the old helicopter landing pads just because we can, buying charity painted shells by the Quay, hoping that the tide works so we don't have the long walk to Carn Near, which is misleadingly far (although it does allow the surreptitious crossing of the heliport) and playing Frisbee on Gimble Porth beach (where champions go to practise) and generally enjoying the freedom from cars and beautiful scenery.

The island is the second biggest in the archipelago and has just under two hundred permanent residents. However, in the summer, the number swells as tourists flock and seasonal workers descend.

Tresco is pretty much owned by the Duchy of Cornwall, and for a long time Wifey and I didn't really like it. In fact, for several years, we didn't even visit. It does have a kind of refined beauty that the other islands avoid. But it has grown on us.

Carn Near quay, Tresco. St Mary's in the background

It started when the girls became old enough to ride bikes. We wanted to tour an island this way, but the traffic on St Mary's, while light by mainland standards, is regular and the roads narrow with high hedged blind corners. But nothing beyond golf carts and tractors is automated on Tresco, so it seemed ideal.

Number Two immediately crashed, but I didn't which is a surprise, since I hold no sense of balance. It was one of my proudest moments that I survived when my seven-year old didn't. Mind you, every time since I have fallen off. It is turning left that does it. And right. And going straight on, when I think of it.

Old Grimsby and New Grimsby are the two towns, on either coast off the centre of the island. There's a sort of island centre, close to New Grimsby quay, where there's a big enough shop, some public loos, the bike hire place and such like.

But it is when you get outside of the 'towns' that the island really comes into its own. Little stone cottages tempt you to sell up and move, there's a pub, and a school, which also caters for younger children from Bryher.

St Nicholas' Church in the middle of the island is steeped in history, as are some ruins. Charles' Castle dates from the middle of the 16th Century, and was occupied by Royalists during the civil war – amazing really that the islands should play any part in this event. A century later Cromwell's Castle was constructed, partly from its older cousin. This is more of a watch tower than actual castle, but still worth a look. Then there is the old blockhouse, up on a hill overlooking Old Grimsby Quay, which again played its part in the civil war.

To stroll along the peaceful, manicured lanes and past the tropical bushes of today's Tresco gives little insight into its turbulent past. The Benedictine Monks whose presence can be seen in the ruins of the Abbey may have brought a touch of peace, but that was a mere eye of the hurricane of trouble which has circulated the island for much of its history.

Problems with Vikings, the armada, as well as the Civil War – whose opposing armies seemed to consider the island little more than a plaything to hold, lose and regain - have troubled Tresco's inhabitants.

In fact, Tresco became a kind of pirates' paradise for Loyalist troops in the 1600s. The greatest battles took place midway through that century, when the Commonwealth side became fed up with Dutch ships being captured and looted. It all became a little embarrassing. The odd English vessel was also privateered.

The battle itself was, by many standards, a tame affair, involving sojourns on Tean and trips between St Mary's and Tresco. It seems as if the weather was the main winner, neither side prepared to venture out in the Atlantic rains unless they had to. In the end, the Royalists were routed, but a generous set of terms of surrender were granted to the Royalist leader on the islands, Sir John Grenville. His troops were permitted to return home, or join other battles and old Sir John himself was even paid compensation for the artillery he left behind.

One of the more notable aspects of this intrusion of war was the foolhardy decision of the Parliamentary side to use locals to row them ashore from their ships. This was to allow their soldiers to land and attack.

Scillonians are great people, generous and funny, but they don't like to be told what to do.

I remember visiting Tresco a few years ago, and there, in the middle of the sound (the shallow waterway around which many of the larger islands are located, was a large blue yacht.

We are talking about avery large luxury plaything, more of a ship than a yacht, in fact. The colour was, and apologies to the owner, pretty horrendous – it was as though B and Q had mis-read the market for dark blue paint and had held a major sale.

The ship yacht, it turned out, belonged to a certain Russian billionaire associated with a west London football club. Perhaps this explained the colour.

'We'll have a little look at that' announced the boatman over the tannoy.

But as we got close to the vessel, it disgorged a handful of tiny launches, which buzzed towards our larger ferry like summer flies around the weeping eyes of an unmoved cow.

'They don't want us here, but I'm going where I'm going,' said the boatmen with a twinkle in his eye.

He set his course and continued, passing within feet of the luxury yacht, while we passengers gazed at the ostentatious wealth. The security vessels quickly retreated, buzzing ineffectually in our direction.

Four hundred years previous to that, the island pilots ferrying soldiers onto Tresco decided it was too rough to land, and diverted instead to Tean, leaving the troops to an exposed night on the tiny outcrop.

Although not much is known about this, it seems as though the Vikings took to Tresco for their own holiday break. The islands were liberated, but contrary to popular belief, Vikings were rarely violent, their raids were quick infiltrations to pillage, but where they hung around, they settled and often advanced the cultures of where they colonised.

It wasn't until the 19th Century, and the arrival of Augustus Smith, that Tresco emerged from its turbulent times.

Smith was unusual, in that he was a Governor who actually lived on the island, most just stayed on the mainland. The diet of limpet and kelp did not appeal.

He set about improving the island, and it has not looked back since.

Bryher – the Hardy Island

A short jaunt across from New Grimsby is the island of Bryher. This little gem is known for stunning scenery and even more notably for possessing the islands' only roundabout. It is a land of many moods.

The southern end is dominated by Rushy Bay, a sandy stretch of beach with calm seas marking the space to uninhabited Samson.

Overlooking Rushy Bay on one side is the mound of Samson Hill which, I know from painful experience, is a tangled mass of prickly bushes. Not a place to visit when the last boat back is due in less than an hour.

We once landed at Rushy Bay, which involved everybody descending a plank attached to the boat's bow and climbing down into a foot or so of sea, then traipsing to the beach. Number two was very young at the time, and I remember trying to carry her over the sea weed, which she, at least, found very funny.

If you choose to avoid Samson Hill, and head the other way, climbing Gweal Hill gives amazing views over rocky outcrops and if you were to dive in and start swimming, the next stop would be Newfoundland. Further to the north is the fearsome sounding Hell Bay, and here the rocks are battered by the Atlantic even on a still day. Views out to the Western Rocks from this side of Bryher tell clearly why there are so many shipwrecks littering the seabed in this region.

Head down the sheltered side of Bryher and the landscape changes. A wide sweeping beach has views over to Tresco, and two quays. The original, Church quay, is at one end, but this is often unusable because of the tide.

The TV personality Annika Rice used to host a TV programme called Challenge Annika, which involved the host working with locals to build some community benefit in a short time, such as over a weekend. The appropriately named Annaquay was one of her creations, and allows greater access to the island.

We were going to call Number Two Bryher, but couldn't decide whether it was a boy's name, or a girl's. I thought male, Wifey female, so in the end we went for a totally different moniker. As usual, it turns out, I was wrong. We missed an opportunity.

Children's writer Michael Morpurgo is a fan of Scilly, and Bryher is his favourite island. A number of his books are set there. Every year we look out for him, unsuccessfully, although on a trip to St Agnes recently we overheard a fellow tourist saying that she had chatted to him the previous day. Very annoying.

Bryher, on a calm day! Look at the sky.

St Agnes – The English Caribbean

St Agnes is our favourite island. The sandbar connecting to The Gugh, our favourite beach. The sun shines more on St Agnes than anywhere else – I've absolutely no evidence for this assertion, nor do I want any, for fear I will be proved wrong. To us it is always sunny here.

We have never had to sit inside for our lunch at the Turk's Head, one of us normally gets a touch of sunburn and we usually get a swim in the lagoon like seas.

There is sometimes a need to dodge the odd jellyfish, but on the sand bar there is a choice of swimming options. Most head for the open sea bay, which is easily accessed and the yachts anchored make for a delightful view.

However, we discovered, quite recently, that the water on the other side, down towards the quay is shallower and warmer. The two are probably connected, although I am no geographer so this, like my assessment of the local weather, is just an anecdotal guess. This bit of ocean is also quieter, because access means taking the barefoot pain dance across rocks – the kind are that big enough to hurt, but small enough to wobble in an ankle breaking, highly dangerous way when stepped on.

On the open side, sometimes there might be, oh, more swimmers than you can count (on the fingers of one hand, that is) whilst we have only once had to share the quay side lagoon.

Close by St Agnes is the island of Annet, which is a bird sanctuary and generally not open to the public. Here, up until mid-July or so, puffins take over. The closest we can get is one of the boat tours which eventually land on the island's larger, inhabited neighbour. We haven't done that yet, it is on the wish list.

There are things to do on St Agnes. A visit to the maze lets you see, really, the most astonishingly unremarkable tourist attraction, and is worth a trip just for that. I am sure that the history is stronger ('It is' says the wife, who knows about these things), but one gets the overwhelming sense that it was created by a couple of bored ten-year olds one afternoon. If it was, then well done to those children, although they would have been, I am informed, medieval children, since the maze is believed to date back to those times. Perhaps the most remarkable thing is that such an unremarkable thing is still around.

The view from St Agnes to The Gugh, technically the smallest inhabited island, at least when the tide's in.

There is the Old Man of Gugh, a three-metre-tall stack which is believed to have been used in Bronze age burial rights. On the Atlantic side of the island, there is the chance of finding shipwreck treasure lingering on the beach at Beady Pool, and Periglis Beach is brilliant for shell collectors.

But the reason it is our favourite island is because it is best for a laze on the beach, lunch and a stroll around the gorgeous lanes to spy the quaint cottages and dream of living in paradise.

St Martins – The Island with the Best Views

An endless St Martin's beach

We've heard of one horse towns, well St Martin's is a one road island. The single carriageway links Higher Town in the higher part of the island, with Lower Town, in the lower part.

Half way between, mid-way up the hill, or down it if you are travelling that way, is Middle Town. It is an island on which it is impossible to get lost.

The views from this road are some of the best on Scilly, especially when the tide is out and the sun is shining.

A giant beach stretches all the way along the inner side of the island, with views of the other major land masses in front. On the open, Atlantic side, things are rougher, but amazing views to Round Island (it's quite round) make a short trek definitely worthwhile.

Tides dictate that pick up and drop off are always (in our experience) at the quays on different ends of the island. You tend to hope that the first stop is Higher Town. Here, you can have a bit of rest on the beach, wander past the world's most attractive cricket pitch and have an early lunch at Little Arthur's café, or buy a picnic from the island bakery.

Thankfully, the journey to Lower Town is downhill.

There are café's, the tiny school, a modern island hall and flower farms to pass through. A stop off at the church is worth a thought. But most of all, the views are magnificent. Enjoy them.

There's a pub in Lower Town, The Seven Sisters, and a rather fine hotel, the Karma, more of which later.

Finally, as you await your boat ride home, simply rest on the beach, overlooking nearby Tean.

Tean, a very special island for our family

Chapter Five: Our Own Odyssey

The islands lay in the path of the gulf stream, a warm ocean current which originates in the tropics. It is why tropical flowers bloom so readily on Scilly, and also accounts for its better than usual weather when compared to the mainland.

There have been countless times when we have watched the July and August weather forecast predicting cloud and rain, and shared a little smile among ourselves. Often, we have sat on the beach, our skies blue but in sight of the heavy cloud in the distance. Frequently, it stays there all day, and we know that Cornwall is suffering, while we swelter happily.

Yet despite its micro-climate, it does rain from time to time, and Scilly is also renowned for its mists.

Newquay Airport, a fine place to spend a wet afternoon

We play a little game on such days called 'Can we hear the planes flying?' You can play it too, because we haven't issued a copyright. It is a little more fun than Exploration, but, to be honest, although it can take a whole day to play, we accept it's got limited appeal.

I can't think of any of our ten years of family visits where there hasn't been at least one day where flights were seriously delayed, or cancelled altogether.

But despite this, we had, until visit number ten, never experienced this ourselves. Well, now we have, and it is a story that must, for reasons of catharsis, be told.

It didn't start well. We were travelling south, full of anticipation. Number One had consumed three packets of polos, and was trailing Number Two by a couple, so the car was full of sugar and excitement induced hysteria. My SATNAV was warning of a major hold up on the M5, 45 minutes delay, it was saying. But there was no quicker alternative. The decision, and I so hate making those, was whether to trust the device, or risk getting off and winding around North Devon lanes to re-join the motorway closer to Exeter.

Number Two was a touch out of control by this time, and Wifey hates flying, especially in the tiny Skybus Jumbos, and was by now suffering from acute stress. (It is a sign of how much we love the islands that she goes through this every year.) By the time I had made a decision, which was to make no decision, it was too late for a decision. We had reached the hold up.

As it turned out, no decision was the right decision, because the queue cleared within ten minutes. The lesson here is never to trust a SATNAV.

Like so often with motorway hold ups, we never discovered the reason for the delay. One of the great mysteries of life, are traffic jams on our fastest roads. So, anyway, we arrived at Exeter in plenty of time, parked as always in the car park just over the way and walked, each with our luggage, into the airport.

We had become used, over the years, to the Skybus desk opening just a few minutes prior to departure, so were pleasantly surprised when we saw the 'Desk Open' sign, and less surprised that there were no holidaymakers in the queue. After all, when the maximum number of additional passengers to us is 13, and we have yet to fly in a full plane, queues at check in are rare.

So, with confidence, we navigated the barriers and headed to the desk. There are not many of these at Exeter airport, but it is a sign of Scilly that, whilst the barriers to other check in desks twist and turn in just the way they do at busier airports, the line to the Scilly desk is marked by a simple, straight corridor.

I should just add, at this point, that the weather was good. The forecast had been fine, and the Devon skies were a mixture of blue disturbed by the odd, largish, grey cloud. But these were high, and we anticipated the sort of journey where Dartmoor,

Bodmin and St Michael's Mount would be visible. We would see the Eden Project, and I would participate in my annual self-imposed challenge to identify Land's End Airport from the sky (still no success).

The first clue that all was not as it should be came as I led the way to the desk. The young employee was looking at her screen, and scribbling something. She did not look up, and it took three gentle coughs before she realised that there was an eager family waiting.

Finally, she looked and registered the sort of surprise that comes when you deal with about one family an hour.

'Oh,' she said. 'I'm not open yet.'

'That's not what your sign says' I wanted to respond, but didn't, because it is never wise to anger airport staff. Instead, I smiled and turned to the family to impart the news. This was of course, unnecessary as they were less than a step behind me, but I find establishing the hierarchy of who's in charge useful in public. Even though everybody knows the order goes Wife, children, dog (even though he stays in kennels) before me.

Now, we were on a 10.00 flight, or thereabouts, and by this time it was about ten past nine. OK, the desk should be open, but as I said above, it was no real surprise that it wasn't. We retired to the small number of hard plastic seats which the Departures section of Exeter Airport offers to keep its customers satisfied, and waited.

Our arrival clearly meant something to the Exeter staff, because within ten minutes, the departure board changed, with the perturbing information which promised, 'Information at 9.30'. Others arrived, and sat, and soon the airport was full (it really is very small).

Next to us were a lovely family – with children, mum, dad (I shall call them Jill and George), granny and hyperactive grandad.

Initially, he offered us entertainment as he sat, emptied his bag, took a phone call very loudly (he wore one of those headsets which require the wearer to feel the need to appear important), made a phone call, walked to the single shop, bought nothing, came back, emptied his bag again, made another call – you get the idea.

Nine Thirty came and went (causing hyperactive grandad to leap to his feet and seek out somebody who would know what was going on – but they had all gone for an elongated coffee break).

By 9.50, when we should have been receiving a repeat of the safety messages from a co-pilot, there was still no news, but then the promised update came. 'Flight Delayed' it said, 'Further Update at 10.00.' Even calm and kindly George and Jill started to make the sort of unspoken eye contact which said that things were not as they should be.

Well, you can guess what happened then. Hyperactive grandad became even more distraught, and started unpacking other members of his party's bags. We moved ours, and got Number Two to sit on them.

When the next announcement came to say that the next update would be at 10.30, it was already 10.45 and we were all getting a little worried. To say the least.

A game of cat and mouse ensued, as passengers sought information, and Exeter staff avoided giving any. The Scilly desk had long been abandoned, but we passengers were made of clever stuff, and positioned ourselves by every entrance, and also in queues to far off destinations such as the Costa Brava and Tenerife.

But the staff were more experienced (considerably more experienced, we later learned) and even if we did catch them, they would use one of two tactics. Either, they would smile, and say that they didn't deal with Scilly flights, but Marion or whoever, would be at her desk soon.

When we pushed on this, they would offer to go backstage and find out more details. Of course, we never saw them again. In defence of Skybus here, because I don't want them to think that we are unfair, the Exeter staff were employed by the airport, not the airline.

By now, the airport was full of passengers on the 10.00 and the 10.30 flights, while the early birds of the 11.30 were also there. We displayed various levels of stress – total frustration from the likes of us, through to concern for the 10.30 flyers and a kind of accepting tolerance from the 11.30 group.

Oh, would they regret their complacency!

At around 11.00 a breakthrough came. Somebody had information. We should await a further announcement, but our plane was still trapped on Scilly, where, apparently, the worst fog of all time had descended. It was as though the islands had been swallowed by the Atlantic.

Now, this was a bit of a mistake, because the Exeter staff forgot that Scilly tourists are frequently on first name terms with landlords, restaurant owners, bar staff and such like. There is also a live webcast running continuously from the islands.

It took only a few moments for us – we were now a team – to discover that Scilly was clear, and flights were expected to start taking off soon.

We relaxed. An hour from St Mary's to Exeter, and we should be on our way within 90 minutes maximum. Annoying, but one of the crosses to bear for choosing to avoid the notorious Scillonian.

Then, at 11.45, bombshell.

Passengers from our flight were called to the desk. We were not worried, a pincer movement earlier had trapped an airline worker, and she had revealed, in return for free passage to her coffee, that flights would be re-arranged in the order that they were due to take off.

Clever. A believable, even common sense, answer but, we were about to discover, completely untrue.

Now, at this point your author was only moments away from incurring the wrath of the airport staff. But I have a defence. We were about to be told that the flight was cancelled, and we should make alternative plans.

Wouldn't most people expect to be offered the options, all together, have a few moments to discuss with family and suchlike, then report back to the airline desk with their decision?

Well, that's what I thought. So, I joined another couple at the desk, aware of the other flyers grouped behind me.

'If you would like to stand back then this lady can let me know of her decision.' The words were sternly spoken, and I looked around before realising it was me, the inconvenienced customer, to whom the attack was addressed. 'If you do not move now, I will have you arrested, or perhaps even shot, if the mood takes me' her look continued.

Having reflected, I realise that choosing whether to go by Scillonian the following day or hope for a later flight is pretty private stuff, if that decision got out, well, therapy at least would be needed so I apologised the lady concerned, and every other assistant at the airport. Let it be recorded in the public annals of the three of so copies of this book that sell, that the Exeter airport staff are the most polite, helpful group of people I will ever have the joy of meeting.

We would have rather been playing Exploration, but then, who wouldn't?

So, eventually, like a naughty schoolboy, it was my turn to face 'Marion'. 'Your flight has been cancelled' she said, in well-rehearsed form, 'You can travel by Scillonian tomorrow, or we can put you on a flight in the morning.' The smile that followed this diktat was also well rehearsed, but it was a brief piece of acting, and her normal bored/angry expression soon returned.

Her pencil did not actually tap as I digested this information, but her look clearly said 'Sad old man' which, to her youth, I probably am.

The thing is, the forecast for the following day, indeed the rest of the week, was not great. Wifey and I had actually congratulated ourselves for our foresight in booking the flight, months before, on the only clear morning forecast for days.

What to do was not a decision I could make alone. The choices were to put my darling wife on a boat that would render her ill for at least 48 hours, or risk the whole family stuck in Exeter for who knows how long. But, to leave the queue could mean waiting until every Scilly bound holidaymaker would be seen before I could offer our choice.

I frantically broadcast across the room to where the rest of the family were waiting, waving to get their attention. Wife came up, but we were both quickly dismissed.

'Oh, take this,' moaned Marion dismissing us with a look and an A5 booklet.

Defeated, I headed to the family but Wifey, who is made of stern stuff, joined me as reinforcements as we went back to further discuss our options.

Re-joining the queue, we soon got to the front. Since nobody was allowed more than 20 seconds to make their call, pretty much everybody had retreated to their families to discuss the options available.

'Scillonian or flight' we were told, as though such a decision was easy enough for anybody but idiots like us.

We raised the question of what would happen if the next day's flights were also cancelled. A shrug was deemed enough of an answer, although eventually we were given the ground-breaking information that, if we were worried, we should book on the Scillonian.

To the questions of how we would get there, and if that had to be achieved by driving the ninety minutes to Penzance, how we would get our car when we flew back after our holiday, we were given the exasperated answer 'Do you want me to book you on the Scillonian or a flight?'

We went for the flight option.

Grumbling, we went back to our base, the children desperately hoping that their holiday might not consist of the free table tennis outside the terminal and occasional tours round WHSmith.

Wifey began to read the booklet while I tried to think of a good way of spending the night in Exeter.

Then, the 10.30 flight was called. I looked sympathetically at my new friends as they went to receive the news. If our flight was cancelled, and we would be the first to get on the next flight available, then the 10.30 had to be off.

Up they went, and within seconds their bags were loaded through check in and they moved off to security.

It doesn't take much to get the Incredible Hulk angry, and it is a character defect that I can be the same. My ire was raised even more when Wifey read that we should have been offered free transport to Penzance for the Scillonian.

Jill and George, trying to cope with young children and hyperactive grandad, asked what we were doing.

'I'm going to ring Skybus!' I announced, like Churchill confirming the Normandy Landings.

'And I'm going to ring my brother, he's already on St Mary's' added George, my new Montgomery.

George quickly ascertained that Scilly was clear, and planes were both landing and taking off.

I discovered that, contrary to the information given, there were seats on the afternoon flight, although it would mean going via Newquay.

'We'll take them,' I said.

'Good, because we've cancelled all flights this morning' the helpful man from Skybus told me. I didn't have the heart to tell him to expect an incoming shuttle shortly, as the 10.30 headed Scilly-wards. Instead, I enquired about the 11.30, passengers of which had by now jumped ship to our 10.00 flight army.

'Oh, that's been cancelled already.' came the reply.

I spilt the beans. The passengers were not happy, and the airport denied it. For another ninety minutes.

So, we waited. The small café was already out of food, the girls were living off Pringles and chocolate from the miniature Smiths.

But at least we were soon to be on our way.

We passed through security a couple of hours later, alone, everybody else had by now resigned themselves to a trip on the Scillonian and a night enjoying the thrills of Exeter. Which are, I am sure, considerable, and my own dismissal of its joys are purely influenced by my experience of the airport, and its staff. I'm certain, as well, that some of these are delightful, helpful people. Statistically, some have to be.

There was a small panic as we waited to board, having watched (for the 19th time) the safety video.

We were sent back to join the passengers of the next flight, which clearly did not have room for four more flyers. Our panicked questions were met by un-reassuring smiles and huddled discussions, but we did board our plane.

Skybus HQ had done us proud. Their claim that the Skybus operative at Exeter would help us no longer niggled – there was no such person, or if there was, they weren't going to admit to it.

The sun was shining and, in an hour, we would be on St Mary's.

And, we had our own private flight. We took off in light, broken cloud and arrived half an hour later in Newquay where another eight or so people joined us. As to why the other five seats had not been offered to fellow passengers, now sitting in the Exeter Travel Lodge, is a greater mystery than I can solve.

But off we went. Into cloud. Then rain. Then, an announcement by the pilot. St Mary's was no longer safe to land on, and we were heading back to Newquay, where we would stay the night.

What we learned over the next hour is that Skybus owns more planes than might be imagined, as it seemed as though they all landed, one by one, at Newquay. The Exeter flight we had feared we would be joining landed soon after us. It turned out that they had got as far as their approach to the landing strip on St Mary's before being turned back.

Newquay staff were very helpful, and as frustrating as it is to sit watching the rain pound, they at least gave us information and booked us hotels for the night.

There, we were advised to book onto the next day's Scillonian, there was no guarantee when the next plane seat would become available.

The Scillonian – board if you dare, although my own experience was really good.

That their airport was now full of empty Skybus planes which could fly us out in the morning didn't seem to occur to anybody with the power to enact this. And when the point was raised, they just said that the planes were not going to the Islands. But we were tired from our campaign, and a new battle was beyond us.

Now, I am sure that Newquay is a splendid place. But on a wet July night, following a day of frustration, its appeal wavers.

I am not going to name our hotel, because the staff were great. But it did have a surreal quality. Firstly, we were offered a five-bed room – yes, five – but the girls are teenagers, or close to, and need their privacy. So, we were allocated the said room, but also another for the girls.

Access to them meant passing through what appeared to be a council meeting in a back annex, which was slightly embarrassing, more so when we traipsed back, wet bags in tow, to say we couldn't find the rooms. Our third interruption was met with less smiles as we realised that the numbering of the rooms followed no logical order.

By the time we went through for the fourth time, to find something to eat, we needed an armed guard.

With the rain pouring and every other building apparently boarded up, we negotiated the penny arcades and came across a well-known Pizza chain. We were after an express meal, so went for it.

Well, back home, and on trips to London, we often eat here, the food is good and there is plenty of choice for the girls.

But the message had not reached Newquay. The 'local' beer was cloudier than St Mary's and the Bruschetta had clearly been cooked in ocean water, it was so salty.

Number Two's lasagne had been left too long in the sun and the pizzas were soft.

The next day, we boarded the bus to Penzance and, with fear in our hearts, boarded the ship.

I think at this point I should affirm that different people have varying levels of tolerance when it comes to seasickness. To me, the journey was brilliant. The rocking was mild – it had turned out, in true Scilly fashion, to be a day that defied the weather forecast. The air was bracing and I loved the crossing. The girls were fine too. But, like the many grey faced passengers,

Wifey took it badly, spending the journey throwing up below deck.

For we intrepid failed flyers, the Scillonian represented a chance for reunion, since all of us from Exeter airport where on it. We shared war stories while the more fragile members of our new community tried to find the least rocking part of the boat.

It would take a day before my Darling was back to normal. But we had arrived, twenty-four hours late, but with the promise that all expenses and the difference between the cost of flights and ferry would be refunded.

Ha, ha.

Well, we had a great time tracing our refund. On the advice of Lynne, our landlady, we popped into the Skybus building to claim our money, but were told that we needed to complete a form for some of it, so could collect our money in two parts, or wait for it all to be despatched from head office.

We decided to wait.

On the morning of our return to home, déjà vu hit.

Scilly was fine, but the mainland wasn't and the planes could not get to us. Then the weather deteriorated further. The Skybus staff at Scilly airport were wonderful, and quickly made the call that, whilst head office might not yet have cancelled, they were going to before long. Therefore, we could choose to take the boat, or get on a flight the following day.

Most passengers went for the Scillonian option, but that was no good for us. The crossing, followed by a long, uncomfortable bus journey and a four-hour drive home was too much to contemplate.

But here's the difference between St Mary's and Exeter. We were sent off, with the promise that if any flight did take off that day, they would hold a place for us. We had some lunch, phoned the airport but there was nothing.

We hit a bit of a problem – some planes were now coming in, but none were going back to Exeter – accommodation on Scilly is hard to find at the best of times, and now there was none.

It became an adventure, searching for rooms. We found one at the rather fancy St Mary's Hall Hotel, which we could not normally afford but our refund would cover. Then, The Wheelhouse – and what a lovely couple run that – found a room for the girls, who were excited at spending a night away from us.

(So were we, but hopefully, they will never find out.)

The following morning, we got a phone call from the airport. We were booked on two separate flights, due to take off ten minutes apart. But one had technical problems. With no fuss, they had sorted us out, and were holding an even earlier flight to replace the one that was certain to be either delayed, or cancelled.

'We thought you'd been through enough trouble,' they said.

And that, I suppose, is the difference between Scilly and the rest of the world.

We did eventually get our expenses, but it was tough, and only came about when Skybus decided that dealing with the ombudsman would be more expensive than accepting our claim.

Technically, Skybus may have been right. They initially refused to pay the difference between the cost of flights and the cheaper ferry, explaining that their responsibility was to get us to the islands. But, as we said, in that case at least give that information to the passengers.

And find somebody with better PR skills at Exeter airport.

(PS – we later found out that there had not been an undisrupted week of flights from Exeter to Scilly that summer. By the time of our holiday, the staff at Exeter had dealt with weeks of disruption, and their patience had word thin. It is not much of an excuse, but we offer our sympathy).

Chapter Six: Twelve Things You Have to Do on Scilly

In no particular order, and from our totally subjective viewpoint.

Number One – Have an evening meal at the Karma, St Martin's

I am a bit conscious that much of this book has centred on eating, (and moaning about Exeter airport.) So, unless I forget, this will be the final mention of food.

Karma is an international, luxury hotel group and lifestyle brand, with destinations off the west coast of Australia, Bali, Thailand and so forth.

It took over the St Martin's hotel and completely refurbished it, staffing the hotel with locals who can offer great advice to tourists.

But our suggestion doesn't quite apply to guests of the hotel, or even those staying on the island, because there is a part of the experience which thrilled the children (and us adults, if we are honest) that it is as important as the wonderful meal the Karma will serve you.

That is, hiring a boat and getting a private ride back to your host island.

The setting summer sun, breeze and crashing over the waves is such a joy, that we actually thought that Number 2 would bounce, laughing hysterically, into the sea.

Number Two – Hire A Scilly Cart

The Eight-Seater from the Scilly Cart Company

The Scilly Cart Co is based in Hugh Town, and driving licence holders can hire a cart for anything from two to eight people. Booking in advance is essential to be sure of getting a vehicle. In fact, it is best to book a couple of months before you leave for your summer break.

One of the main joys of Scilly is that you can easily walk anywhere, but a cart for the day is a treat. We found that we quickly covered all aspects of St Mary's, our carefully structured itinerary abandoned because the girls loved riding in the back, facing following traffic. (OK, I admit it, I loved driving around as well. The 12mph speed limiter seemed much faster with open sides blowing the wind through).

But after an hour or so, we thought we had better set up some sort of plan or the battery would be flat. So, our day consisted thereon of a trip to the golf course for a game of bowls (it doesn't make this list, but give it a go.) We felt like royalty arriving by cart, although, sadly, there was no red carpet marking our patronage.

We had a coffee in the Kaffee Hause – I'm not allowed to say much, because of the rule about food above, but the coffee and hot chocolate are great, although the café is a fair way off the beaten track, even for Scilly. Replenished, we drove on, via every road on which we were allowed to drive, to the Carn Vean. A walk down to Pelistry followed, then on to an afternoon at Old Town bay. We managed one more island tour before the battery showed signs of flagging. A great day.

It was interesting, as well, to see St Mary's from the perspective of road users. As holidaymakers, we tend (as do many) to use roads as a kind of extra wide path. We shouldn't, it's dangerous. We could meet a driver like me.

Number Three – Halangy Down

This is our favourite ancient settlement. Iron age, which means it dates from about 200BC, although above the old village is a large, partially restored, burial chamber which dates from around 300 years earlier. That, as historians will know, makes it bronze age.

There are various other sites and chambers littering the islands, the one at Innisidgen well sign posted and definitely worth being part of any coastal walk itinerary. Cynical children might be under-whelmed (our intelligent, interested prodigies excepted, naturally) but if you save the walk until well into your holiday they will have become in tune with the fact they are not in Disney.

Apparently, the main islands did not become separated until about 1600 years ago, St Agnes apart. It was then that centuries of gradually rising and eroding sea levels pierced the horseshoe shaped land mass and created what we see today.

In fact, as any old timer will know, there are a couple of times a year when Crow Sound (the waterway between St Mary's and St Martin's) dries up because the tide is so low. It is possible, with the help of somebody who can read the soggy sand, and who is quick enough, to start on the north St Mary's coast, cross to St Martin's, along the coast to Lower Town and, via Tean and St Helen's make it all the way to Tresco.

A bit of wading later, Brhyer can be conquered.

This land mass was, in Cornish dialect, called Ennor, and sitting on Halangy Down it is incredibly easy to slip back over 2000 years and imagine being part of the life of the islands in those days.

The village is still laid out, with some stonework showing. Look out and the ancient fishermen are there on the shore line.

Number Four – Seal Snorkeling

Our eldest bought me a seal snorkeling trip for my birthday a couple of years ago. It turned into a family event. Give it a go if you get the chance.

We made our way on the company's boat to St Martin's, donned wet suits and life jackets, and were immediately bouncing across the Sound and round The Arthur Islands. Seals are abundant.

Close up, it's a surprise how big they are. Our crew spent some time choosing a spot for us, then it was flippers on, masks down and in we went.

Two things struck immediately – how vast the sea is as you look out, head only fractionally above the swell, and sometimes below it. You can just see, bobbing up and down as you tread water, a distant mainland. Secondly, how impossible flippers make any kind of movement.

Getting friendly, a Scilly seal

The first of these concerns was easily solved by turning around and realising that the back end of Little Arthur was a mere few metres away. As for the flippers, I never came to terms with these.

Then the seals appeared. They are an inquisitive bunch – I guess I should have realised by the frequency which curious heads pop up off the beach at Pelistry – but in their habitat, they get up really close.

Their favourite habit is to nibble at flippers – they could have just taken mine, to be honest.

We spent a good while in the water, and it was apparent that our guides were on first name terms with most of these blubbery mammals.

I think what struck me most was how perfectly at home in their environment they were, and how not were we. I was going to add that they don't have to put up with flippers, but of course, they do.

Number Five – Visit a Gallery

The islands are littered with crafty places. Bordeaux pottery on the road between Old Town and the airport is a wonder of bowls and plates, vases and animals. John, the owner, is as interesting as his work, and will regale you with tales of the islands.

Last time we were there, we got talking about the helicopters, or lack of them. The conversation had started, as I recall, by John asking us how many times we had been to the islands. This often-asked question involved a long answer, with lots of sub clauses. The children, at this stage, were on their ninth trip, for me it was 10, and for Mrs P about 18. Which inevitably led to the question of how we got here – tales of Scillonian horrors are a local currency – and the disappointment that the helicopters no longer ran.

British International Helicopters had provided the service since 1964. The company sold its Penzance base, from which it flew to both St Mary's and Tresco, to Sainsbury, and planned to use the funds created to buy newer aircraft and an updated site.

However, according to the company, Tresco and two private individuals had threatened legal actions against them, and the risk of delays made continuing the service untenable.

Following much head-shaking on all sides, John moved on to tell about a major helicopter tragedy that had occurred just a little over thirty years previously.

That had been a major news story, at the time the biggest loss of life in Britain from a helicopter crash.

16th July 1983 was the kind of day when Skybus planes would stay firmly grounded. Heavy mists came and went, and stretched right down to sea level.

Many passengers used the helicopter service between Penzance and St Mary's, and it could cope with worse conditions than planes. For various reasons on the day, the helicopters were being flown by pilots whose familiarity with the route was limited.

The crash was put down to pilot error. He was flying low to cope with poor visibility, and misjudged the height of the craft. It turned out, as well, that the pilot had not made sufficient checks of his instrument panel.

The crash led to a number of changes to the rules around flying commercial helicopters, the most significant that it became mandatory to have audible height warning equipment fitted.

Imagine that, only a tad over thirty years ago, and a helicopter could fly in an area noted for its misty weather without the back up of an audible warning when it got too low. And that helicopter was permitted to carry passengers.

When bad things happen, it is often a combination of events that causes the problem. Confusion appeared to reign on this occasion. The investigation revealed that the pilot and co-pilot had interpreted information from another helicopter flying back to Penzance in different ways.

They were flying at 500 feet, able to see the sea below, but not much in front of them. They then descended to 250 feet on their approach, checked instruments for a final time and, confident that they were now below the cloud base, concentrated on flying by visual guides.

Under two miles from landing, with clearance from the St Mary's airport, the pilots believed they were still flying at 250 feet. In the passenger compartment, the attendant told passengers that they were at 100 feet.

In fact, they were at zero feet, and crashed into the sea.

Floats were fitted to the aircraft which should have provided stability in such an event, but they immediately broke off and the helicopter balanced on the surface, leaking water.

Stability was lost, and the aircraft flipped and sank. Only six people got out. These were the pilot and co-pilot, two children and two women. None had time to don life jackets, and the pilots kept the group afloat by using suitcases.

The lifeboat was launched ten minutes later, and search and rescue instructions were given. A navy helicopter was first to arrive, but even though it was flying directly above the group, the fog was so bad that it could not see them.

After an hour in the water, the lifeboat – its crew using the smell of aviation fuel to bring them close to the survivors – arrived, and the six were taken on board. It seems as though the company did not learn lessons. Although it disputed the claims, a journalist took a flight in the days following the crash, and reported that there were several failings with safety systems.

Passengers walked around the craft even when the seat belt sign was on, ticketing was not named and the safety announcement was inaudible.

On my first trip to the islands, I flew by helicopter. It was very stable and enjoyable, but extremely noisy.

It seemed, according to the crash report, that 20 people had died because of the pilot had made a mistake, unintentionally descending and crashing when he thought he was flying well above the waves.

The accident report concluded that conditions were unsuitable for visual flying because, bluntly, the weather was too bad to see very much at all.

John tells the story much better, focussing much more on the emotional impact on the islanders. It clearly affects many older Scillonians still.

We reflected for a moment, then bought two splendid bowls, which grace a blanket box at the top of our staircase. Such is life.

Every island features sheds and shops selling home produced art work and crafts. Often, they are just left open, untended (presumably, the owner off being creative somewhere). A real favourite is North Farm Cottage gallery on St Martin's. It is along a small offshoot of 'The Road', near the bakery.

Inside, paintings and nick-knacks tempt, but it is the freshness of everything that attracts us.

We always spend a half day at the Phoenix craft studios, to produce our own pieces under the guidance of Oriel, the highly skilled glass decorating owner. Our house is adorned with stained glass creations from Wifey, she is very talented; and mugs, plates and roundels from the girls.

These mark, rather poignantly for us these days as our girls grow up, milestones in our lives, each item being made a year after the last.

The early plates are decorated with heavy squiggles of paint, but gradually designs become identifiable and then increasingly ornate. They are as effective as photographs at plotting our children's move from infancy to teenage-hood. We'll always hold on to them.

Sorry, time to pause and wipe a tear of nostalgia for those early childhood years which won't ever return.

Number Six – Swim off Samson

Regular Scilly goers will be familiar with the islands' most famous sport. I don't mean gig racing, although this is a popular summer past-time. No, I mean their 'Confuse the Tourist' game. The leaders of this piece of fun are the island boatmen who pilot the ferries running from St Mary's to the off islands.

Experienced players can gain a head start by reading the boards which list the times and boats going to particular islands, but even then, a touch of chance is involved. You see, the quay at 9.45 in the morning is extremely busy. Usually, there will be one of the ferry boats in, already heaving under the weight of sun seeking island hoppers.

Samson at Sunset – we have a picture of this amazing island hanging up at home

That will always be headed to Tresco. But as for the other islands – well, your boat could be anywhere. There are at least four more docking points along the quay – one right at the end and one, cleverly, tucked out of sight on the near end by the ticket office.

The game then follows this pattern. The family will arrive and look out into the harbour for their boat, then scan along the quay edge. There will be four or five queues formed. The family (you can play it solo, but it works better with a group) then walk slowly down the tarmacked strip, hoping that they will spot their boat coming in.

An added factor here is the joker of several boats looking very similar. For example, is that red hulled beauty coming in the Sea King, or is it Surprise? While you are deciding, gamblers and those with better eyesight will have nipped in front of you.

Usually, having lost twenty places, you discover that it is neither and in fact you still have no idea where your boat will dock, so you tag on to the end of a queue at random. Then, trying to appear as unidiotic as possible, give an apologetic smile and ask: 'Do you know where this queue's for?'

One of three answers follow:

1) St Martin's

2) We hope it's to St Martin's – this can be delivered with varying degrees of confidence.
3) No idea.

This is such a clever game, because the players then need to work out how trustworthy their information supplier might be. Unjustifiably over-confident? Lacking in self-belief?

As I said earlier, there are clues the experienced player might employ – the board tucked on the side of the Atlantic Inn. The full boat for Tresco (don't worry if you can't get on it, they always run extras). Another clue is the boat already docked but with no queue and just half a dozen souls on board.

That will be headed for Bishop's Rock or The Eastern Isles. I dread the day some super whizzo time and motion person arrives and makes finding their boat easier for the holidaymakers. Half the fun will be lost at a stroke.

But there is one destination where there is never a need to play this game. That is if you are headed out to Samson. Just look for the boat with a tiny dirigible attached to the back.

Because Samson is uninhabited. The last hardy residents left in the 1850s.

Getting to Samson is tricky. Sometimes the tides are wrong and landing is just impossible. If the weather looks bad (PS – the Met Office should move to Scilly – locals are always right, to the minute) then, as there is absolutely no shelter anywhere, the trip will be off.

But if all is well, then get on board and, after usually a brief drop off on Bryher, you will soon be there. If you are really lucky (or unlucky, if you were looking for the dirigible) then you get to walk the plank.

This involves a wooden plank attached to the front of the boat, down which you walk to the beach. Or a foot of water. Hint – never wear long trousers when going to Samson.

The plank thrills the children, of course. One year, it also thrilled a lady who, alone apart from a large black lab, was determined to be first down the plank. Barging small children and picnic carrying parents out the way, she ascended the bow, where the dog took one step onto the plank and promptly sat down.

Nothing would move it. This was some stubborn dog. Nobody could get past. The lady was completely unabashed, laughing lustily after her pampered pet, and pointing out to the dozen or so others of us how funny it was.

Unfortunately, after twenty minutes, the joke wore thin. The dog was carried by the Captain and his Assistant back into the boat, and we descended. In the end, the dog dived into the water and swam ashore.

We buried it, and its owner, in the well on the island. The bodies will never be discovered.

But usually, hanging on to the side of the tiny inflatable, landing happens. The island has a large beach at the north end, which twists round to face Bryher and Rushy Bay ahead. Its twin hills make it identifiable from anywhere on the islands, and the ascent of each is easy. Between the hills is the island well, then ruins of the houses begin, and continue up the second hill. Again, they are very much worth looking at, and give a great insight into the toughness of living on a tiny settlement in pre-industrial times.

Seven families lived there at its population peak in the 1820s, but by 1855 only two families remained – the Woodcocks and the Webbers. But they were suffering badly, not least from living on a diet of limpets and potatoes. Augustus Smith removed them to a bigger island, and Samson became uninhabited.

Smith created a deer park, but even these got off as soon as they could, wading to Tresco at low tide.

Private boats pull up throughout sunny days, and there is a narrow strip of water at low tide, which lies between the main island and a sand bar which gradually gets revealed. The water in this narrow strip is deep enough to swim, and always warm. Honestly. The perfect place for a dip.

It's like your own Coral Island (or, if the kids get bored, Lord of the Flies.)

Number Seven – Any One of the Other Uninhabited Islands

Annet apart, if you hire your own tiny boat, a number of islands beckon. I have never seen a trip listed to land on any of the Eastern Isles, although sometimes a small boat might be spotted, and a lone figure spied on a quiet beach, but the twelve islands that consist of this range remain largely untouched for many years.

However, there is evidence of Bronze Age through to Roman settlements. Nornour, (and isn't that the best name?) holds the clearest evidence, with round houses, a brooch factory and a shrine to a Roman Goddess all present. I don't know if I will ever make it, but a visit to Nornour is my number one ambition. At least, now seal snorkeling and driving a Scilly Cart have been achieved.

But there are two more islands that will from time to time be accessible on a planned. organised trip. These are Tean and St Helen's, and I urge you to go.

Head to Tideline, a shop in the centre of Hugh Town and you will see a board advertising Calypso II trips. Often, these are three islands in a day, but if you ask to speak to Tim, who runs the boat, and if he can get enough business, he will take you to St Helen's and Tean.

Tean is very close to St Martin's, and at very low tide you can walk across. It is a low island, with a single old cow shed and house. It is really two islands, which separate at high tide. Rarely will you find anybody else on it, and it is stunningly beautiful.

As is its name. Could there be a finer moniker to give your child? As well as several houses carrying the name, when on Scilly you will, from time to time, hear 'Tean' (pronounced Teee-Ann, with an umlaut over the 'a') called to a pretty girl. There are not many Teans about, but they are all very special.

Tim's boat, find his board (and a great array of nick-nacks) at Tideline

There's evidence of settlements and graves from Roman times and back to the Bronze age, but of course the island would not have been such then. There's also evidence of an early Christian Chapel on the island.

However, in the 1600s a house, the only one, was lived in by the Nance family. They were kelp burners, an activity which creates the substance needed to make glass, sodium carbonate.

It is not the most efficient method of making glass, and needs a lot of kelp – but that is not a problem on Tean. However, by the mid-1800s, better methods had been found, and the kelp industry, consisting of one family, ceased.

Tean is interesting geologically, as it was shaped by the ice age, and for those to whom this is of fascination, contains lots of glacial evidence. Yay.

Nearby St Helen's is, in our view, less pretty but possibly of more historical interest.

Apart from wandering around the island, there are three exciting things to do on St Helen's.

First of all, are the remains of an 8th century Christian site in which St Lide lived. It developed from a small hermitage to a tiny community, with evidence of agricultural development. There was also a church, believed to date from the 13th century.

Secondly, is the Pest House. Enter the remains and you immediately get a sense of being a sailor far from home, taken to this tiny island, almost certainly to die. Parliament instituted a law in 1754 which required any ship heading to England with sailors suffering from the plague to set them down the island.

A quay was built, and near to the house is the grave of a naval surgeon sent to treat the ill. He lasted less than a week – probably not a job that provoked many volunteers.

The final treat of St Helen's is to be attacked by herring gulls. They nest in large numbers, and are aggressively protective. Those who enjoy living on the edge should be aware of their established attack routine, which involves squawking, walking from side to side, swooping overhead (really, move away if they reach this point), pooing on you and then, finally, full on attack.

Australia might have its redback spiders and box jellyfish, and Florida its Great White Sharks. Trust me, they are a walk in the park when compared to a herring gull attack.

Number Eight – Bishop's Rock

There are a number of lighthouses surrounding Scilly. The numerous wrecks littering the coast give just cause for their presence.

Personally, I think that the one of Round Island is the most dramatic. Built on an enormous lump of granite, north of St Helen's, landing with materials was just about impossible. Today, the steps cut into the sheer cliffs are still there, although arriving by helicopter is the way the lighthouse is maintained.

But Bishop's Rock, made famous by the BBC2 programme linking video, runs it close. Most days, when the weather allows, one of the Scilly boats will run out, beyond Annet and St Agnes, to the giant, spectacular edifice.

By the time the boat arrives, you are in serious Atlantic waters, and even on the calmest day the vessel dips and rises. The lighthouse is built on a granite outcrop, and marks a long ledge just below the surface to which many ships have succumbed. However, the outcrop on which the lighthouse is built rises sheer from over 100ft down, and the prospect, in the mid-1800s, of building such a monument was thought impossible. The force of waves and wind would simply blow the construction away. And those tasked with building it. (Maybe GP at the St Helen's pest house doesn't sound so bad.)

Cleverly, they came up with the idea of building it on legs, so the wind would pass between them, rather than against the construction. All started well enough. But, just before the lighting element could be fitted, a storm happened and it was goodbye light house.

However, the building's engineer, James Walker, was made of stern stuff, and over the next eight years the granite block lighthouse we see today was constructed. Building was slow, the blocks had to be shaped to add strength to the construction, and access to the outcrop was limited by the weather. The construction crew were housed on a nearby islet – accommodation was built there, in the middle of the Atlantic. It must have been a fun job.

But, within a few years, the structure was unsafe again. A new base was constructed, which gave some protection by absorbing the force of waves, and the lighthouse was made higher, to its current height of almost 50 metres.

These days it is automated, but still, from time, has workers staying. The BBC 2 video shows arrival is by helicopter, with workers landing on top of the construction. I hope than none suffer from vertigo.

To see it close up confirms the lighthouse as one of the wonders of British engineering. Plus, the trip out is great fun, and the boat driver will offer all kinds of observations, facts and, when the opportunity arises, point out the amazing bird and sea life en route.

Number Nine – Walk Round the Garrison

You should feel safe on the Garrison, it's been the island's protective presence since the late 1500s. Over the years, further fortifications have been added until now the promontory above Hugh Town, which is called The Hugh, is completely walled in.

The Garrison, head here in case of attack from Tresco

The Spanish Armada prompted the building of the first section of wall, to stop the islands from becoming a safe haven from storms for invaders from the West.

It was still active as a defensive position as late as the second world war. The Garrison's greatest use, though, came in during the Civil War, when the prince who would become Charles II hid on the island, before escaping to Jersey. With no one to protect, the Royalists surrendered to the Parliamentary forces, but not for long.

800 men were stationed there, when the Royalists retook the base two years later. It would swap hands once more, though, after Admiral Blake captured Tresco (as we saw earlier, not without a fight) and launched a thunderous attack which forced another surrender.

The massive batteries which are still to be seen inside the walls were mostly installed at the end of the 19th Century, and the thousand soldiers stationed there during World War One must have felt they had bought a winning lottery ticket, both avoiding the horror of the trenches, whilst being camped on the beautiful, warm and friendly islands.

Second World War Pillboxes can still be seen, and the Garrison became a surprisingly important part of the Battle of the Atlantic, operating as a signals station.

There are two entry points to the Garrison, the main one is through the massive arched gate up the hill from the quay. More exciting is a hidden passageway located between two of the giant terraced houses at the top of Hugh Town.

You need to search for this entrance, as it looks simply like a stairway up to the houses, but creep below them, through the tunnels, and suddenly you emerge inside the Garrison walls themselves and there, you see immediately why the spot was chosen to defend St Mary's.

Apparently, parts of the Eastern walls are closed to the public, although I can't say we've ever noticed. For us, the Garrison now provides a valuable cardio vascular service. Wifey and I will get up, leaving the girls to laze in bed, and carry out a brisk walk around the Garrison on a morning. Cutting through the tunnels, which are closer to us than the arched gate, we briskly circulate, with me stopping us to admire the amazing views (across to Samson is my favourite) when the pace gets too much.

Towards the end of our sojourn (past the playground which the girls used to use) we pass Star Castle, the fortification built in 1593 which is now St Mary's most luxurious hotel. We've never stayed there, primarily because the thought of climbing the steep rise after a day on the beach is too much. That we can book our lovely Custom House for a fortnight for the price of couple of nights in the hotel does not bother us at all, of course, and plays no part in our decision making.

After all, who really needs amazing food, brilliant views, a luxurious setting and the kind of comfort the best hotels offer? Not us, that's for sure. Definitely. Completely out of the question. Not in the spirit of Scilly at all.

Number Ten – Museum

The Scilly Museum, located between Town and Porthcressa beaches, offers a fine way to spend a wet afternoon.

Our girls loved it, although, they were only about eight at the time. Lots of local life is represented, and it offers a great way to get more out of your own explorations of wrecks, wildlife or the ancient settlements.

The museum is, like the islands themselves, a bit of a throwback. There is little that is interactive. You enter, are faced with a varied and packed collection of fascinating artefacts, which you look at and read about…then (and here's a novel idea for the younger generations) you talk to your family and friends, discussing what you have seen.

Visitors learn, and have fun because that.

Look, I don't want to come across as a complete dinosaur here. I have a mobile phone, and can use some of its features. But sometimes I think that technology has gone too far. It takes away mankind's social skills, and replaces them with overactive thumbs, false understanding and fake friends. I know this is not original thinking, but it needs to be said. It's dumbing everything down, making people feel important because they can vote in some stupid interactive poll. Well people, that technology is not freeing you, it is imprisoning you.

Marx described religion as the opium of the masses, that's no longer the case (if it ever was), now it's technology.

Sorry, but I had to get that off my chest. I feel better now. Thanks for listening.

Number Eleven – Buy a Book

To have reached this point, you've already done this, and I thank you from the bottom of my heart, and my other organs which, thanks to your kindness, I have not had to sell on the Dark Web. But, I mean a more serious book.

If you have children, then Michael Morpurgo features the islands in Why the Wales Came, and the Wreck of the Zanzibar. Both are great stories, and you can look on Bryher and Sampson for the places he writes about.

Visit Man o' War opposite Holgate's Green, Mumford's newsagents or Bordeaux for a selection of Scilly's best. Slightly off topic, but Number Two is a devourer of books, and given that the luggage allowance is so small on Skybus, we take her card and make use of Scilly's own library, which is to be found just behind the playground end of Porthcressa beach.

If it is still available, and I am sure it will be, Life of a Scilly Sergeant, is written by Scilly's own chief of police Colin Taylor (sadly, now back to fame on the mainland). As well as disabusing the reader that crime never happens (although, that which does tends to pretty low key) he tells great anecdotes about, for example, chasing drunken drivers on a kid's bike.

Number Twelve – Old Town Church

The tiny church is dark and delightful, dating from the 12th century but it's really the churchyard that demands attention.

As you pick your way through the falling stones, history unfolds in front you. Victims of ship wrecks – there is a huge obelisk to one such traveller, which dominates even the war memorial. Those who died on the SS Schiller, which sank in 1875, are especially numerous. The names of locals are still the ones we hear today – Hicks, Mumford and such like.

In one of the newer additions to the graveyard, in a grave of remarkable ordinariness lies Sir Harold Wilson. At the time of writing, his wife Mary, 101 years old, was still an occasional resident, her plain bungalow on the outskirts of Hugh Town.

Harold, twice Prime Minister of the United Kingdom, loved the islands and retired to St Mary's in later life.

Guarding the Wrecks – Bishop's Rock Lighthouse

Chapter Seven: Everything Else

I have become, as this book developed, aware of how little I know about Scilly. Although it seems that I have been visiting forever, when I actually look at it, I have spent about five months in total on the islands.

It is a sign of the friendliness and welcome that Scilly gives that I, like many others who come back year and year feel like we belong.

Like many, we have considered long and hard moving full time to the islands. But, each time we think of taking the plunge, the remoteness pushes us back.

So now, as I reach the end, I am forced to think about so much that has been missed.

Sir Cloudsley Shovell

Has there ever been a better named Admiral? Stern of face, podgy of middle and with the flowing locks of a 1980s footballer, Sir Cloudesley is buried in Westminster Abbey. However, he died as a result of the Western Rocks, and washed up on Porth Hellick, where a small plaque, overlooked by the Scilly Camel, marks where he was found.

Sir Cloudesley – no emerald ring in sight

As would be the case for any leader of his day, Cloudesley came from a wealthy background. He grew up in Norwich, but his family connections to the Navy meant that he left for sea while still in his early teens.

Cloudesley was his grandmother's surname, and presumably he was glad to be away from a family that would load him down with such a moniker.

He became a mid-shipman when seventeen and saw action early on. It seems as though he was a capable chap, presumably having developed a sense of resilience from a young age, fighting off comments about his name (about which, I promise, no more will be said).

Variously described as the 'best officer of his age' and 'beloved of sailors' he was a knight of the realm and an admiral when in his forties. He commanded the naval element of England's involvement in the War of the Spanish Succession, leading the fleet to Barcelona in 1705.

Two years later, he was again in charge as British ships attempted to capture Toulon. The campaign failed, although the French lost a number of their own fleet. Shovell sailed home, with the knowledge that the French were no longer a force in the Mediterranean, even if he had failed in his mission to capture Toulon.

He was heading towards Plymouth when westerly winds drove him towards Scilly. The fleet was trapped overnight on the treacherous seas amongst the even more dangerous rocks. Shovell's flagship, the Association, struck Outer Gilstone Rock and sank. All on board died. In fact, three ships sank that night, and out of 1300 sailors, only one survived.

Rumour has it that Shovell was still alive when he washed up on Porth Hellick Cove, and was killed by a woman who stole his emerald ring. She confessed on her death bed, and the ring was sent to a friend of the admiral, the Earl of Berkeley.

Although she may well have taken his ring, the villainous witch, it is unlikely that Sir Cloudesly was still alive. Surviving the watery journey, in horrendous conditions, all the way from Outer Gilstone Rock to Porth Hellick Cove would have been a remarkable feat.

Other Shipwrecks

The islands are littered with wrecks, many of which foundered on the Western Rocks. Here are a few with a story to tell.

One of the earliest recorded was in 1305. The name of the ship is unknown, but as was the usual manner in those days, the islanders went to salvage the cargo. A coroner, William Le Poer, took charge of this, but was imprisoned by the Lord of the Manor on Tresco, and forced to pay for his freedom.

In 1617 a ship survived being wrecked on the Western Rocks. A part of the East India Company, the pinnace Supply was driven aground. The cargo and the men on board were rescued, and the ship was repaired before returning on her adventures.

Almost thirty years later, a Royalist ship, John, ran ashore after involved in a fight with three ships supporting Parliament. These were the days of the Civil War, and the pirate John Mucknell was on board, taking advantage of the situation.

In fact, over time too many have wrecked on Scilly for this little book to record. However, a trip to the Hugh Town shops mentioned earlier will provide lots of choices for those wishing to make a bigger study. The 1800s saw rates increase, as the use of ships for cargo and passengers became more widespread, although it may just be that we have more details because record keeping was better. 189 ships at least were wrecked, lost or at least mildly injured in that century.

It was from the shipping industry that the gig racing for which Scilly is yet another world leader (along with food, beaches, beauty and so on) began. Gigs would rush out to larger vessels to offer to pilot them through the treacherous rocks that threatened to sink the unwary. The first to arrive would secure the job.

Naturally, when a ship ran aground, or floundered, the same gigs would speed to offer help. And, when the situation allowed, offer to look after the cargo. Permanently.

Some examples of sinkings from the 1800s and onwards include the full rigger, Horsa, which had made it all the way from New Zealand before Bread and Cheese Cove in St Martin's did for her. Although no men were lost, the ship needed to be towed to be repaired. Sadly, she did not make it, capsizing near Bishop's Rock.

There are some happy stories, however. When the London based steamer, Egyptian Monarch, had nearly arrived home from New York in 1888, she became stranded off of Bryher. She was carrying passengers and cargo, but happily managed to be refloated, after which she finished her journey.

Off to find a shipwreck, on board the Firebrand

1888 was a bad year, with several sinkings. Bernado, an Italian vessel, crashed into Annet, presumably disturbing the puffins which should have been beginning to arrive. The Captain was rescued, and the ship's figurehead – St Bernard – is still to be found on Tresco.

1881 was even worse, St Jean, Charlotte Dunbar, Kron Prinz von Preussen, the SS Culmore, Independenzia and Excelsior all met their watery graves. The last of these looked as though it could be saved. It beached on the very shallow Crow Bar, which lies in the waters between the islands. It eventually drifted on to St Martins. Repairs took place, and in January 1882, the ship left St Martin's shores to continue its journey. However, the repairs did not hold, and it quickly sank.

Disasters followed with similar regularity during the first part of the 20th century. The SS Minnehaha, however, was one of those lucky few that survived their collision. She hit Scilly Rock off Bryher when in heavy fog, but was refloated. This ship was a first-class liner, and unlike the Titanic in two years' time, all survived.

The First World War saw a number of wrecks, some as a direct result of conflict, and World War II produced similar results. German U Boats, waiting to attack Atlantic Convoys, particularly suffered, with at least five being lost during the conflict.

Even with the benefits of modern technology, Scilly still claims the odd boat. In 1977, a French trawler, Enfant Du Bretagne, was lost in the Western Rocks. The lifeboat came close to the crew, but all drowned before they could be rescued.

In 1997 the MV Cita, a German cargo ship, was wrecked off St Mary's. The crew had been sleeping while the ship was on automatic pilot, and all were rescued.

One final wreck is particularly sad, and does not involve a ship. During World War II, some passenger planes still flew from Scilly. A de Havilland Dragon aircraft was flying to the mainland from St Mary's when it crossed the path of a German bomber, which was believed to be returning from a raid in the north of England.

Although the passenger plane was slow moving and clearly unarmed, the German bomber shot it down, and there were no survivors.

For those interested in getting up closer to shipwrecks, it is possible to book a sea safari which will take you to these sad graves.

The St Mary's Boatmen's Association

Ready to load up, some of the brightly coloured boats of the association

The brightly painted boats that will ferry tourists to the off islands, to see Bishop's Rock and Annet, as well as other places of interest, are run by the St Mary's Boatmen's association.

Crossing the sea between the islands in an open boat is thrilling. Journeys are short, apart from visits to the lighthouse at Bishop's Rock, or tours, the trips tend to take twenty to thirty minutes.

They are a humorous and helpful lot. Often the engine will suddenly turn off as the boatmen spots something of interest, which is pointed out to the passengers. Maybe a rare bird, of a group of dolphins.

I recall one of the captains taking a route to Bryher all the way round the back of the island (a brilliant way to see the reason why so many ships have wrecked off Scilly, and why Hell Bay is so called.)

His reason was to show a pair of rare nesting birds. We were not charged extra for the longer and interesting journey, he just thought that we might be interested in Scilly wildlife, which every single passenger was.

Although the Boatman's Association operates out of St Mary's, each of the off islands has its own boat which offer trips to other islands.

The boat owners are very much the heart of the Scilly Isles. They represent families that have been around for many generations, they have adapted their skills as tourism has overtaken other industries as the major source of income to the islands, they are knowledgeable and tolerant of visitors and their questions.

Like the majority of the residents of Scilly, they seek to help and never appear annoyed by the annual influx into their lives. They hold a sense of perspective from which the rest of the world could learn much.

Maybe this is a rose-tinted view, but none of my family care if it is. It is how we see Scilly, and long may that continue.

Chapter Eight – Some Final Words

Many thanks for buying this book. I hope that it has offered an insight into these most wonderful islands from the perspective of a person who spends his annual holidays there.

Number One and Number Two have never asked to go anywhere else. We took a holiday to Florida one year, when they were still just pre-teens. We had a great time, but Number One said, on the way home, that she was glad we still went to Scilly.

There will be much about these islands I have missed. They featured for a couple of years in a TV show called 'An Island Parish', and as entertaining as the programme was, we did fear it might lead to change and greater numbers of visitors.

But however annoying getting to the islands can be, it is that difficulty that ensures they are always relatively peaceful. There are simply not enough ways to get many more visitors to Scilly, and nowhere for them to stay if there was.

And, I know that the views I have offered might be a little romantic – but then we always go when it is summer, and the Gulf Stream is doing its trick. It is the views of a tourist family I have offered.

Living on Scilly all year round is tough, however wonderful two or three weeks a year might seem.

There is little in the way of work for young people, unless they are lucky enough to have a family business into which they can progress. Education is hard. Scilly schools are some of the most successful and high performing in Britain, but they are small. Apart from Bryher, the children of which travel daily to Tresco, when weather permits, each island has a primary school. St Martin's example being the smallest school in England.

But once the children turn eleven, there is only one secondary school on the whole of Scilly. That is a newish, well equipped school. Any child who lives outside of St Mary's needs to board during the week as, should a storm system set in, transport between the islands is impractical.

And, from 16, the only education available is on the mainland.

The islands possess a really well-equipped hospital, but it is inevitably small. Anything beyond the most basic treatment means a flight or boat ride to the mainland. The islands possess a hospital boat, doctors and nurses travel from St Mary's to the off islands, but it is not like having a surgery down the road.

During bad weather, fresh food can be hard to find. The local co-op is the only shop of any size, and if deliveries are not possible, then tins, frozen and dried foods come into play.

There is no cinema on the islands, although films are occasionally shown in other venues. A group of local actors put on the occasional play, and there will be rare visits from visiting performers, but they tend not come in the Summer.

Entertainment is what you can make, and the local pubs.

But for all this, if I could, I'd move there in a flash. When Number One and Number Two have little numbers of their own, we might.

I hope that experienced Scilly visitors will have found some new ideas, or may view their traditional holiday in a new light, having read this book. I hope that they might have their own bucket list of things to do, their own list of favourite restaurants and activities. Email them to me on abpeters@abpeters.co.uk and I will happily publish them on my website.

And for those to whom Scilly was no more than a possible destination amongst many possible holiday spots, I hope that you take the opportunity to visit, and enjoy. You may find yourself coming back year after year. So many do.

I hope that you find your way to the islands, by plane or boat. Or perhaps, if the talk of reinstating the helicopter flights leads to action, by that means of transport. I hope that you see these wonderful islands first hand. That you find the beauty, the peace, the gentle pace, and the ability to put the world into perspective that characterizes Scilly.

But, not too many of you…

Printed in Great Britain
by Amazon